·H·S·P·
CALIFORNIA
EXCURSIONS

Gold Pass
Reader

Grade 2

Senior Authors
Isabel L. Beck • Roger C. Farr • Dorothy S. Strickland

Authors
Alma Flor Ada • Roxanne F. Hudson • Margaret G. McKeown
Robin C. Scarcella • Julie A. Washington

Harcourt
SCHOOL PUBLISHERS

www.harcourtschool.com

ISBN 10: 0-15-375344-7
ISBN 13: 978-0-15-375344-2

2 3 4 5 6 7 8 9 10   0918 15 14 13 12 11 10 09

Gold Pass
Reader

Grade 2

Harcourt

SCHOOL PUBLISHERS

www.harcourtschool.com

Contents

How Rules and Laws Help Us

 Social Studies

 Social Studies

 Social Studies

Lesson Opener 8

Content-Area Vocabulary 10

Law and Order 12
by David Conrad • INFORMATIONAL BOOK

Our Trip to Washington, D.C. 20
by Elizabeth and Paul Baggett • TRAVELOGUE

Lakedale Press: Students Rule New Playground ... 26
by Mona Lee • NEWSPAPER ARTICLE

Comparing Texts 28

Content-Area Vocabulary Review 29

In the Marketplace

Lesson Opener 30

Content-Area Vocabulary 32

Lemonade for Sale 34
by Stuart J. Murphy • illustrations by Tricia Tusa •
INFORMATIONAL STORY

Goods and Services 50
by Janeen R. Adil • NONFICTION

Scarcity 52
by Janeen R. Adil • NONFICTION

Comparing Texts 58

Content-Area Vocabulary Review 59

Social Studies/ Math

Social Studies

Social Studies

The Lives of Animals

Science

Lesson Opener 60

Content-Area Vocabulary 62

Animal Life Cycles 64
SCIENCE TEXTBOOK

Science

Following Lab Directions 72
DIRECTIONS

Animal Mysteries 74
by Vicki Young Park • MAGAZINE ARTICLE

Science

Comparing Texts 76

Content-Area Vocabulary Review..................77

Mapping Our World

Lesson Opener 78

Content-Area Vocabulary 80

Land and Water 82
SOCIAL STUDIES TEXTBOOK

How to Label a Map of North America 90
by Alys Thomas • HOW-TO ARTICLE

How California Land Is Used 92
by Mike Graf • NONFICTION

Comparing Texts 98

Content-Area Vocabulary Review..................99

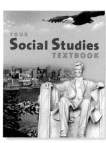

Social Studies

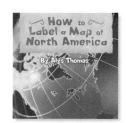

Social Studies

Social Studies

Theme 5 • Better Together

Moving Forward

Lesson Opener 100

Content-Area Vocabulary 102

Science

The Giant Cabbage 104
by Chérie B. Stihler • illustrations by Jeremiah Trammell
FOLKTALE

Two Fables 124

Social Studies

    A Tale of Two Mice 124
    retold by Ermine May • FABLE

    The Ant and the Grasshopper 127
    retold by Ann McGovern • FABLE

From Seed to Pumpkin 130
by Wendy Pfeffer • illustrations by James Graham Hale
INFORMATIONAL BOOK

Science

Comparing Texts 136

Content-Area Vocabulary Review 137

Tracing Our History

Lesson Opener **138**

Content-Area Vocabulary **140**

Grandma Lai Goon Remembers **142**
by Ann Morris • illustrations by Peter Linenthal
NARRATIVE NONFICTION

How to Make a Time Line **154**
by Boyd N. Gillin • HOW-TO ARTICLE

Using a Map Grid **156**
by Jean Gray • HOW-TO ARTICLE

Comparing Texts **158**

Content-Area Vocabulary Review **159**

Glossary **160**

California ELA Standards **165**

Social Studies

Social Studies

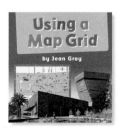

Social Studies

How Rules and

The leaders in our schools, communities, and country make rules and laws. Fair rules and laws keep us safe and help us get along.

In this lesson, you will read

- "Law and Order"
- "Our Trip to Washington, D.C."
- "Students Rule New Playground"

Laws Help Us

Content-Area Vocabulary

R1.6
HSS2.3.1

WORDS ABOUT
Government

law

government

election

Congress

Laws help people drive safely. A **law** is an important rule that people have agreed to follow.

Our government needs good leaders. A **government** is a group of people who run a community, state, or country.

CALIFORNIA STANDARDS
ENGLISH-LANGUAGE ARTS STANDARDS—Reading 1.6 Read aloud fluently and accurately with appropriate intonation and expression. *Also* **History-Social Science 2.3.1** Explain how the United States and other countries make laws, carry out laws, determine whether laws have been violated, and punish wrongdoers.

These children are having an election for class president. When people have an **election**, they vote to choose their leaders.

Our nation's Congress meets in a special room. **Congress** is a group of people elected to make laws for our country.

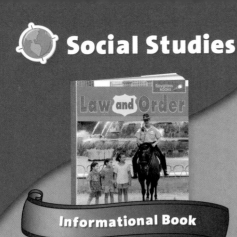

Informational Book

Read to

- understand how laws are made.
- learn who makes sure that laws are followed.
- learn what happens when someone does not follow the laws.

R2.3
HSS2.3.1

Law and Order

by David Conrad

Rules to Live By

"Treat people the way you want to be treated."

This is a rule that helps people live together happily. People live by many other rules, too. The rule to raise your hand before talking keeps the class quiet and makes sure everyone is heard.

Some rules help people stay safe. Some rules help people know how to behave. Rules can only work if everyone follows them. Police are people who make sure that everyone follows the rules. Larger towns and cities may have many police officers.

A crossing guard helps keep children safe.

13

Police in Small Towns

In some small towns, there may only be one or two police officers. This is because there are fewer people than in a big city.

Did You Know?

Sheriff is another name for the main police officer in some small towns.

14

Police in Large Towns

Larger towns and cities may have many police officers. The city may have different stations in different places in the city. In a city, each police officer has a special job. A traffic officer makes sure people follow the rules of the road.

State Police

Each state has its own police department. State officers can work anywhere in the state. The Highway Patrol uses state officers to keep people safe on the roads.

State Patrol officers

Did You Know?

When state police officers are in a city or town, they work closely with the town's police officers.

The Nation's Police

Each country has its own police force, too. In the United States, the FBI, the CIA, and the Secret Service work to protect the country.

Did You Know?

One of the main jobs of the Secret Service is to protect the president of the United States.

FBI training

17

Lawmakers

Every single rule or law was once just an idea. Then the people voted on it. If most of the people thought the idea was good, it became a law.

Did You Know?

Sometimes a law gets old or doesn't make sense anymore. Then people vote to get rid of it.

REGISTRAR-RECORDER/COUNTY CLERK • COUNTY OF LOS ANGELES • CALIFORNIA

Court

When people do not follow the rules, they go to court. Court is where people who break the law find out what their punishment is. Lawmakers, the police, and the courts all work together to keep people safe.

A judge

Think and Respond

R2.5
HSS2.3.1

1. How are laws made? IMPORTANT DETAILS

R2.5
HSS2.3.1

2. Who helps to make sure that people follow the laws? IMPORTANT DETAILS

R2.6
HSS2.3.1

3. What might happen when someone does not follow a law? CAUSE AND EFFECT

CALIFORNIA STANDARDS
ENGLISH-LANGUAGE ARTS STANDARDS—Reading 2.5 Restate facts and details in the text to clarify and organize ideas; **R2.6** Recognize cause-and-effect relationships in a text. *Also* **History-Social Science 2.3.1** Explain how the United States and other countries make laws, carry out laws, determine whether laws have been violated, and punish wrongdoers.

19

Travelogue

R2.5
HSS2.3
HSS2.3.1
HSS2.3.2

Our Trip to Washington, D.C.

by Elizabeth and Paul Baggett

We are visiting Washington, D.C., with our parents. It is the capital of the United States. Today we are learning about our government.

We start here. This is the Capitol building. This is where laws are made.

See the flag on one side of the Capitol? That means that lawmakers are meeting right now.

On our tour of the Capitol building, we see that it is very big. It has lots of rooms. The two biggest rooms are called chambers. One chamber is for the Senate. The other chamber is for the House of Representatives.

Together, the Senate and House of Representatives make up the Congress. Congress votes to make laws.

Right now the people in the Senate have to talk about a bill. Then they will vote. A bill is an idea that would make a good law. The House of Representatives liked the bill. Its members have already voted yes for it.

Senate meeting

Next, if the Senate votes yes, the bill will go to the President. If the President likes the bill, he or she signs it. When the President signs the bill, it becomes a law.

This is where the President lives and works. This is the White House.

White House

Now, we are visiting the Supreme Court building. The Supreme Court is the highest court in our country.

A judge makes decisions in court. Supreme Court judges are called Justices. Justices make sure laws are fair.

Supreme Court Building

Supreme Court Justices

We are almost back to our hotel near Embassy Row. People who live in each embassy come from another country. Their job is to find ways to work together with our country.

See the red and white flag? That is the flag for Canada. This is the Canadian Embassy.

We are having a great time! Washington, D.C., is an interesting place to visit.

The Canadian Embassy in Washington, D.C.

Lakedale Press

DAILY NEWS

R2.3
HSS2.3.1

The school held an election. They elected students to choose playground rules.

Students Rule New Playground

by Mona Lee

Lakedale—This spring, Washington Elementary School got a new playground. Then the school held an election. They elected students to choose playground rules.

"Five students from different grades were in the group," said Jake Cooler. Jake was elected from the third grade.

After the election, each class made a list of ideas for playground rules. They gave their lists to the group.

The group voted yes or no for each rule. In all, they voted yes to four rules. They gave these rules to Principal Harris to approve.

CALIFORNIA STANDARDS
ENGLISH LANGUAGE STANDARDS—Reading 2.3 Use knowledge of the author's purpose(s) to comprehend informational text. *Also* **History-Social Science 2.3.1** Explain how the United States and other countries make laws, carry out laws, determine whether laws have been violated, and punish wrongdoers.

These are the rules he approved yesterday.

The New Playground Rules

1. Students may not jump off the swings.
2. Only one student may go down the slide at a time.
3. Students must go down the slide feet first.
4. Students may not leave the playground.

Jake Cooler feels that getting ideas from students was important. "Our group looked at the list of rules. We talked about them. We voted yes or no on the rules, just as Congress does on laws," he said. "We gave the list to Principal Harris. He signed the rules he liked, just as the President does!"

Principal Harris feels that the students know what is important. "Now we have good rules for our new playground," he said.

Students enjoying the new playground

Social Studies

Comparing Texts

R2.5
W1.1

1. How is the information in all three of this lesson's selections alike? How is the information different?

2. What are some rules and laws that you should follow?

3. How are the students in "Students Rule New Playground" similar to the members of Congress in "Our Trip to Washington, D.C.?"

✏ **WRITE** Why is it important that people follow laws? Use information from "Law and Order" to help you write your answer.

CALIFORNIA STANDARDS
ENGLISH-LANGUAGE ARTS STANDARDS—Reading 2.5 Restate facts and details in the text to clarify and organize ideas. *Also* **Writing 1.1** Group related ideas and maintain consistent focus.

Content-Area Vocabulary Review

Give a Clue

Write the Vocabulary Words on slips of paper. Place the slips face down. With a partner, take turns choosing a slip of paper.

On your turn, look at the Vocabulary Word on the paper and give your partner clues about the word. Without saying the Vocabulary Word, try to get your partner to guess what it is.

Draw It

Choose a Vocabulary Word. Write it on the back of a sheet of paper. On the front of the paper, draw a picture about your word. Ask your partner to guess the word by looking at the picture. Then use other Vocabulary Words to tell about your picture.

WORDS ABOUT Government

law

government

election

Congress

In the

People make choices about how to earn money. They also make choices about how to spend it for things they need and want.

In this lesson, you will read

- "Lemonade for Sale"
- "Goods and Services"
- "Scarcity"

Marketplace

Content-Area Vocabulary

R1.6
HSS2.4.3
M-S1.1

WORDS ABOUT
Resources

resources

consumer

bar graph

scarcity

Our land and water are important resources. The **resources** of a group of people are the things that they need and use to help them live.

This woman shopping for a bag of oranges is a consumer. A **consumer** is a person who buys things or uses services.

CALIFORNIA STANDARDS
ENGLISH-LANGUAGE ARTS STANDARDS—Reading 1.6 Read aloud fluently and accurately with appropriate intonation and expression. *Also* **History-Social Science 2.4.3** Understand how limits on resources affect production and consumption (what to produce and what to consume). **Math-Statistics, Data Analysis, and Probability 1.1** Record numerical data in systematic ways, keeping track of what has been counted.

The bar graph shows which kinds of cookies second graders chose to eat this week. A **bar graph** is a chart that shows changes in how much there is of something.

A long time with no rainfall can cause a scarcity of water. If there is a **scarcity** of something, there is not enough of it for the people who need it or want it.

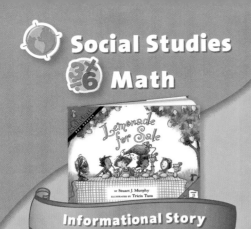

Read to

- understand the role of buyers and sellers.

- understand how buyers and sellers depend on each other.

- find out how you can use graphs to add numbers.

R2.7
HSS2.4.2
M-S1.1

Lemonade for Sale

by Stuart J. Murphy   illustrated by Tricia Tusa

The members of the Elm Street Kids' Club were feeling glum.

"Our clubhouse is falling down, and our piggybank is empty," Meg said.

"I know how we can make some money," said Matthew. "Let's sell lemonade."

Danny said, "I bet if we can sell about 30 or 40 cups each day for a week, we'll make enough money to fix our clubhouse. Let's keep track of our sales."

Sheri said, "I can make a **bar graph**. I'll list the number of cups up the side like this. I'll show the days of the week along the bottom like this."

On Monday they set up their corner stand. When people walked by, Petey, Meg's pet parrot, squawked, "Lemonade for sale! Lemonade for sale!"

Lemonade 25¢

Matthew squeezed the lemons.

Meg mixed in some sugar.

Danny shook it up with ice
and poured it into cups.

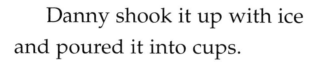

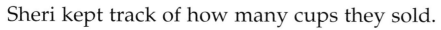

Sheri kept track of how many cups they sold.

Sheri announced, "We sold 30 cups today. I'll fill in the bar above Monday up to the 30 on the side."

"Not bad," said Danny.

"Not bad. Not bad," chattered Petey.

38

On Tuesday Petey squawked again,
"Lemonade for sale! Lemonade for sale!" and
more people came by.

Matthew squeezed
more lemons.

Meg mixed in
more sugar.

Danny shook it up
with ice and poured
it into more cups.

Sheri kept track of how many cups they sold.
Sheri shouted, "We sold 40 cups today. I'll fill in the bar above Tuesday up to the number 40. The bars show that our sales are going up."

"Things are looking good," said Meg.

"Looking good. Looking good," chattered Petey.
On Wednesday Petey squawked, "Lemonade for sale!" so many times that most of the neighborhood stopped by.

Matthew squeezed even more lemons.

Meg mixed in even more sugar.

Danny shook it up with ice and poured it into even more cups.

Sheri kept track of how many cups they sold.
Sheri yelled, "We sold 56 cups today. I'll fill in
Wednesday's bar up to a little more than halfway
between 50 and 60."

"That's great," shouted Matthew.

"That's great! That's great!" bragged Petey.
They opened again on Thursday, but
something was wrong. No matter how many
times Petey squawked, "Lemonade for sale!"
hardly anyone stopped by.

Matthew squeezed just a few lemons.

Meg mixed in only a couple of spoonfuls of sugar.

Danny's ice melted while he waited.

Sheri kept track of the few cups that they sold.

Sheri said, "We sold only 24 cups today.
Thursday's bar is way down low."

"There goes the clubhouse," said Danny sadly.

Petey didn't make a sound.

"I think I know what's going on," said
Matthew.

"Look!" He pointed down the street.

"There's someone juggling on that corner, and
everyone's going over there to watch."

"Let's check it out," said Meg.

Danny asked the juggler, "Who are you?"

"I'm Jed," said the juggler.

"I just moved here."

Sheri had an idea. She whispered something to Jed.

On Friday, Sheri arrived with Jed.

"Jed's going to juggle right next to our stand," Sheri said.

That day Petey squawked, Jed juggled, and
more people came by than ever before.

Matthew squeezed
loads of lemons.

Meg mixed in tons
of sugar. Danny shook
it up with lots of ice
and almost ran out of
cups.

Sheri could
hardly keep track
of how many
cups they sold.

"We sold so many cups today that our sales are over the top. We have enough money to rebuild our clubhouse."

"Hooray!" they all shouted. "Jed! Jed! Will you join our club?"

"You bet!" said Jed.

"You bet! You bet!" squawked Petey.

Think and Respond

1. Who were the buyers in this story? Who were the sellers? MAIN IDEA AND DETAILS

2. How did the club members depend on other people? DRAW CONCLUSIONS

3. How did the club members use a graph to help them add? Give details. IMPORTANT DETAILS

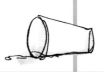

CALIFORNIA STANDARDS
ENGLISH-LANGUAGE ARTS STANDARDS—Reading 2.7 Interpret information from diagrams, charts, and graphs; *Also* **History-Social Science 2.4.2** Understand the role and interdependence of buyers and sellers of goods and services; **Math-Statistics, Data Analysis, and Probability 1.1** Record numerical data in systematic ways, keeping track of what has been counted.

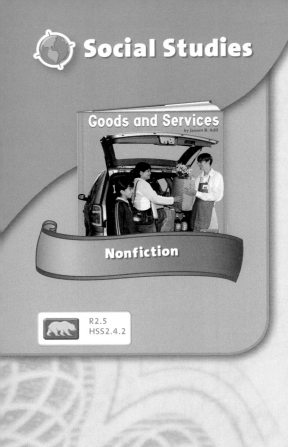

Goods and Services
by Janeen R. Adil

Nonfiction

Goods and Services

by Janeen R. Adil

People buy things they need and want. They buy goods and services. Goods are real things that people can touch and use. A service is work done for other people. An eye doctor does a service as he checks your eyes. The glasses he sells are goods.

Goods and services are sold by producers. Farmers sell the vegetables they grow. Mechanics are producers. They sell the service of fixing cars.

Kids can also be producers. Tim sells a service when he delivers newspapers. He can also sell the cookies he baked.

Anyone who buys and uses goods and services is a consumer. Consumers choose what goods and services they buy. Jenna is a consumer. She uses her money to buy a new bike.

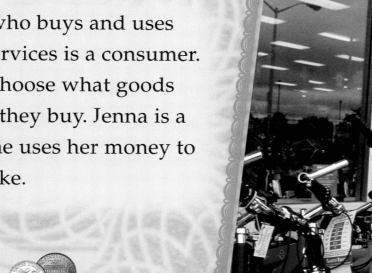

Producers earn money, or income. Mary is a producer. She sells candy in her shop to earn money. Then she uses her income to buy goods and services from others. Mary is a consumer when she buys meat from the market.

What goods and services do you buy?

HSS2.4.1
HSS2.4.3

Scarcity

by Janeen R. Adil

What Is Scarcity?

These three girls each want an orange, but only one orange is left. Not all the girls can get what they want.

Things people want and use are resources. Just like these girls, people want more resources than they can have. There aren't enough resources for everyone. This is called scarcity.

CALIFORNIA STANDARDS
History-Social Science 2.4.1 Describe food production and consumption, including the roles of farmers, weather, and land and water resources; **HSS2.4.3** Understand how limits on resources affect production and consumption (what to produce and what to consume).

How Scarcity Happens

All resources can be scarce, but some resources become more scarce at times. For example, cold weather can harm orange trees.

Then farmers have fewer oranges to pick and sell. Oranges would become scarce. There wouldn't be enough oranges for everyone.

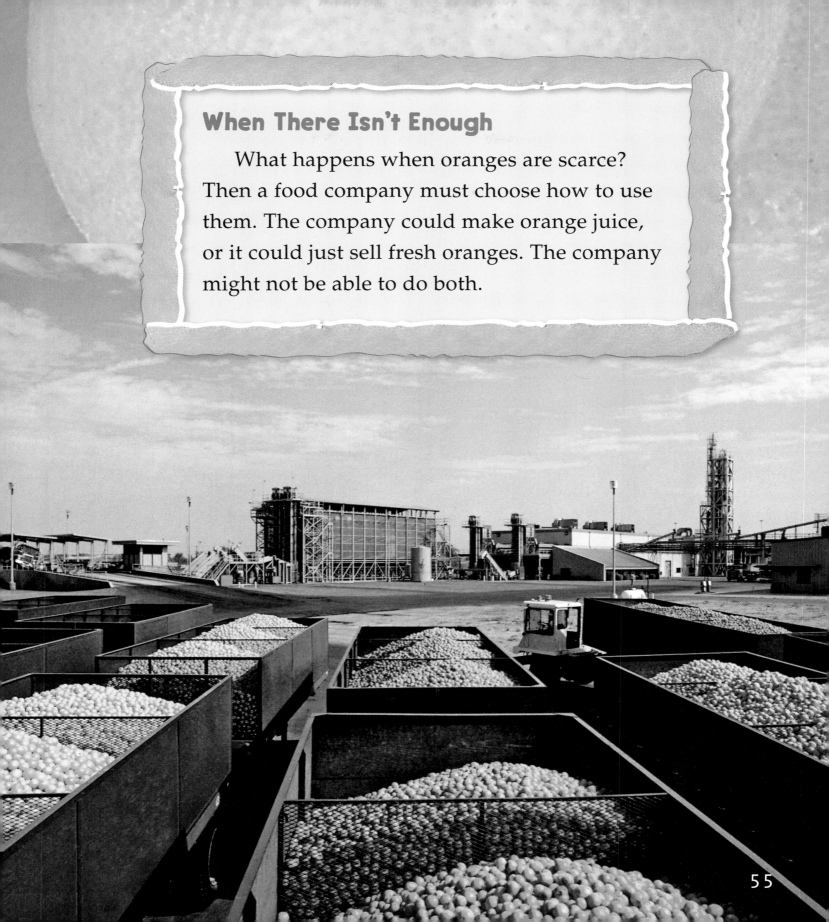

When There Isn't Enough

What happens when oranges are scarce? Then a food company must choose how to use them. The company could make orange juice, or it could just sell fresh oranges. The company might not be able to do both.

Prices

If oranges are scarce, not everyone can have them. But many people still want oranges.

Stores raise the prices of scarce items. Oranges cost more money when they are scarce. If people want the oranges, they must pay a higher price.

Making Choices

Scarcity means people have to make choices at the store. If oranges are scarce, what are the choices? People can pay a higher price for the oranges. They can also try to find a better price at a different store. They could buy another fruit instead.

What would you do if what you wanted to buy was scarce?

Comparing Texts

R2.5
W1.1
HSS2.4.2
HSS2.4.3

1. How are the members of the Elm Street Kids' Club in "Lemonade for Sale" like Mary in "Goods and Services"?

2. What is something you can do to be a producer?

3. If something is scarce, would many people be able to buy it? Why or why not?

✏ **WRITE** How can someone be a producer and a consumer?

CALIFORNIA STANDARDS
ENGLISH-LANGUAGE ARTS STANDARDS—Reading 2.5 Restate facts and details in the text to clarify and organize ideas; **Writing 1.1** Group related ideas and maintain consistent focus. *Also,* **History-Social Science 2.4.2** Understand the role and interdependence of buyers (consumers) and sellers (producers) of goods and services; **HSS2.4.3** Understand how limits on resources affect production and consumption (what to produce and what to consume).

Content-Area Vocabulary Review

Give a Clue

Write the Vocabulary Words on slips of paper. Place the slips face down. With a partner, take turns choosing a slip of paper.

On your turn, look at the Vocabulary Word on the paper and give your partner clues about the word. Without saying the Vocabulary Word, try to get your partner to guess what it is.

WORDS ABOUT Economics

consumer

resources

bar graph

scarcity

Draw It

Choose a Vocabulary Word. Write it on the back of a sheet of paper. On the front of the paper, draw a picture about your word. Ask your partner to guess the word by looking at the picture. Then use other Vocabulary Words to tell about your picture.

The Lives of

Just like people, the animals around us grow and change. The stages, or times, of their lives make up their life cycles.

In this lesson, you will read

- "Animal Life Cycles"
- "Following Lab Directions"
- "Animal Mysteries"

Animals

Science

Content-Area Vocabulary

R2.7
SCI2b

WORDS ABOUT
Animals

environment

life cycle

larva

pupa

The pond is this bird's environment. An animal or plant's **environment** is all the things around it that can help it or make it hard to live, like air, water, and other animals and plants.

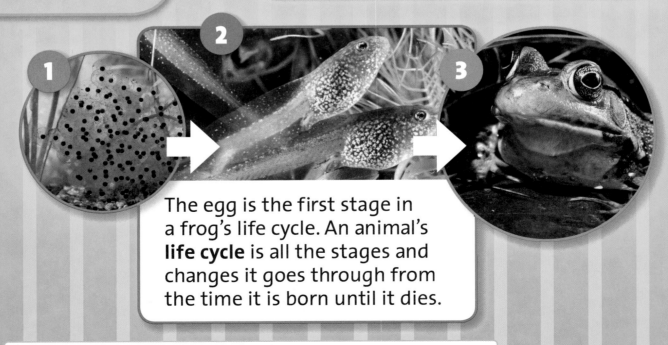

The egg is the first stage in a frog's life cycle. An animal's **life cycle** is all the stages and changes it goes through from the time it is born until it dies.

CALIFORNIA STANDARDS
ENGLISH-LANGUAGE ARTS STANDARDS—Reading 2.7 Interpret information from diagrams, charts, and graphs; *Also* Science 2b Students know the sequential stages of life cycles are different for different animals.

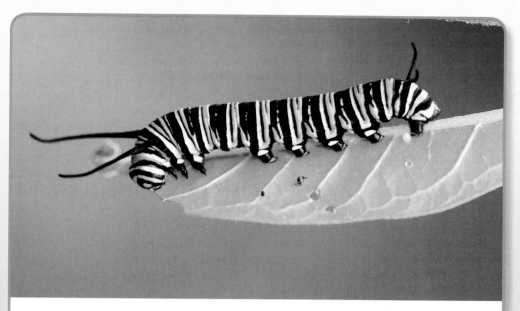

A caterpillar is the larva of a butterfly. A **larva** is an early stage of an insect's life when it looks like a short, fat worm.

A caterpillar becomes a pupa and makes a hard covering. A **pupa** is a stage of insect life between larva and adult when the insect is in a hard covering and does not move.

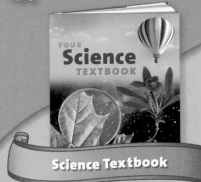

Science Textbook

Read to

- learn about and compare animal life cycles.

- understand how young animals look like their parents.

- learn how animals change in the environment.

R2.5
SCI2a
SCI2b
SCI2c

Animal Life Cycles

All animals have a life cycle. A **life cycle** is all the stages in an animal's life. Different kinds of animals have different life cycles.

Life Cycle of a Butterfly

A butterfly is an insect. A butterfly's life cycle has four stages. The first stage is an egg. Its next stage is **larva**. The larva is a tiny caterpillar that hatches from the egg.

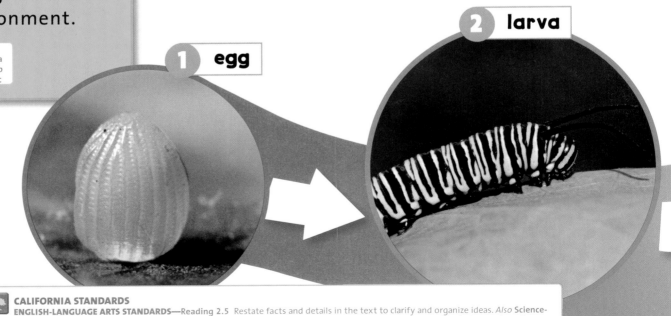

1 egg

2 larva

CALIFORNIA STANDARDS
ENGLISH-LANGUAGE ARTS STANDARDS—Reading 2.5 Restate facts and details in the text to clarify and organize ideas. *Also* **Science-Life Sciences 2a** Students know that organisms reproduce offspring of their own kind and that the offspring resemble their parents and one another; **SCI2b** Students know the sequential stages of life cycles are different for different animals; **SCI2c** Students know many characteristics of an organism are inherited from the parents. Some characteristics are caused or influenced by the environment.

Then the larva becomes a **pupa**. A pupa makes a hard covering. It grows and changes inside the covering. Last, out comes a butterfly! A butterfly can have young of its own.

Question What happens first, next and last as a butterfly grows?

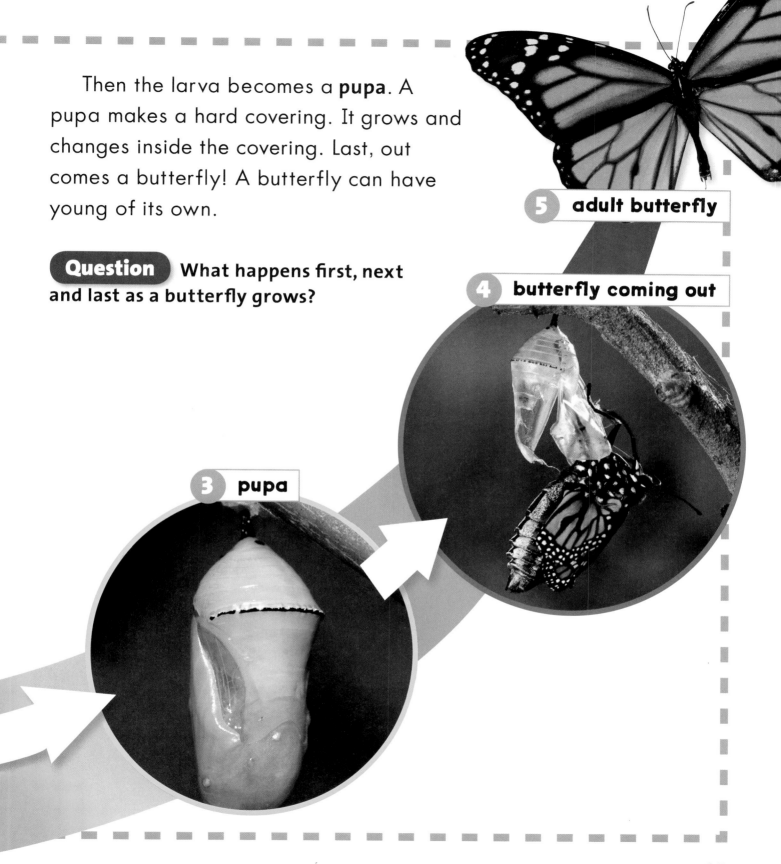

5 adult butterfly

4 butterfly coming out

3 pupa

Life Cycle of a Cat

A cat is a mammal. It has a life cycle like other mammals. First, kittens grow inside a mother's body. Then they are born.

The mother cat feeds her kittens with milk from her body. She watches over her kittens and keeps them safe.

1 adult cat and kittens

2 kitten about 3 weeks old

The kittens grow for about a year. They get bigger and stronger. They become adult cats. An adult is a full-grown animal.

Question What happens first, next, and last as a cat grows?

3 **young cat about 6 months old**

4 **adult cat**

Animals Are Like Their Parents

Animals have young that are like their parents. They have the same appearance, or the way they look. For example, a kitten will have the appearance of a cat. It may have fur like a dog has, but it will not look like a dog.

Many young animals also act like their parents. They move in the same ways. They eat the same kinds of food.

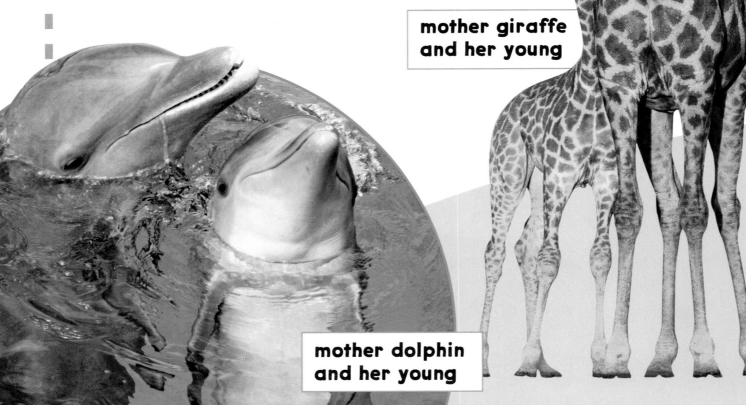

mother giraffe and her young

mother dolphin and her young

Animals Are Different From Their Parents

Even though animals are like their parents, they are not exactly like them. Their color may be different. They may grow larger or smaller than their parents. They may become stronger or faster.

An animal's parents may be different from each other. Their young may even be different from each other.

Question In what ways can animals be like and different from their parents?

Yorkshire terrier

poodle

poodle-terrier puppies

Animals in the Environment

Animals look and act like their parents. But the environment also affects how they look and act. The **environment** is all the things around them.

The weather is part of animals' environment. A cold environment can affect the way animals act. It can also affect how they look.

squirrel in summer

squirrel in winter

In the fall, some animals such as squirrels grow thicker fur. Their fur will keep them warm in winter. They also eat more in fall to store food. Storing food helps them live through winter when not much is growing.

Question How does the environment affect some animals?

Think and Respond

R2.5
SCI2b

1. What is the life cycle of a cat? How is it different from a butterfly's life cycle?

COMPARE AND CONTRAST

R2.5
SCI2a

2. How can young animals look like their parents and yet look different, too? DRAW CONCLUSIONS

R2.5
SCI2c

3. How are some animals different in the summer and winter? MAIN IDEA AND DETAILS

CALIFORNIA STANDARDS
ENGLISH-LANGUAGE ARTS STANDARDS—Reading 2.5 Restate facts and details in the text to clarify and organize ideas. *Also* **Science-Life Sciences 2b** Students know the sequential stages of life cycles are different for different animals; **SCI2a** Students know that organisms reproduce offspring of their own kind and that the offspring resemble their parents and one another; **SCI2c** Students know many characteristics of an organism are inherited from the parents. Some characteristics are caused or influenced by the environment.

Following Lab
Directions

Directions

R2.8
SCI2a

Following Lab Directions

Labs are little experiments in your science book. They give you directions to do something. They help you explore by doing.

Read the labs on these two pages. Use reading strategies to help you. Tell how the directions are the same and different.

Mini-Lab 1

Dogs and Puppies

Using paper and markers, draw a mother dog, a father dog, and two or three of their puppies. Then compare your drawings with a classmate's. How are the parents and their young the same? How are they different?

CALIFORNIA STANDARDS
ENGLISH-LANGUAGE ARTS STANDARDS—Reading 2.8 Follow two-step written instructions. *Also*
Science-Life Sciences 2a Students know that organisms reproduce offspring of their own kind and that the offspring resemble their parents and one another.

Mini-Lab 2

Dogs and Puppies

Materials

- paper
- crayons
- markers

Directions

1. Draw a mother dog, a father dog, and two or three of their puppies.

2. Compare your drawing with a classmate's. How are the parents and their young the same? How are they different?

Magazine Article

R2.7
SCI2a
SCI2b
SCI2c

Animal Mysteries
Do You Know the Answers?
By Vicki Young Park

This is the same fox in winter and summer. Why is the fox white and then brown?

fox in winter

fox in summer

Answer: This fox lives in the Arctic, where the land is covered with snow in winter. It has white fur then, so it cannot be seen easily. In the summer, its fur changes to brown or gray. It blends in with the ground around it.

CALIFORNIA STANDARDS
ENGLISH-LANGUAGE ARTS STANDARDS—Reading 2.7 Interpret information from diagrams, charts, and graphs. *Also* **Science 2a** Students know that organisms reproduce offspring of their own kind and that the offspring resemble their parents and one another; **SCI2b** Students know the sequential stages of

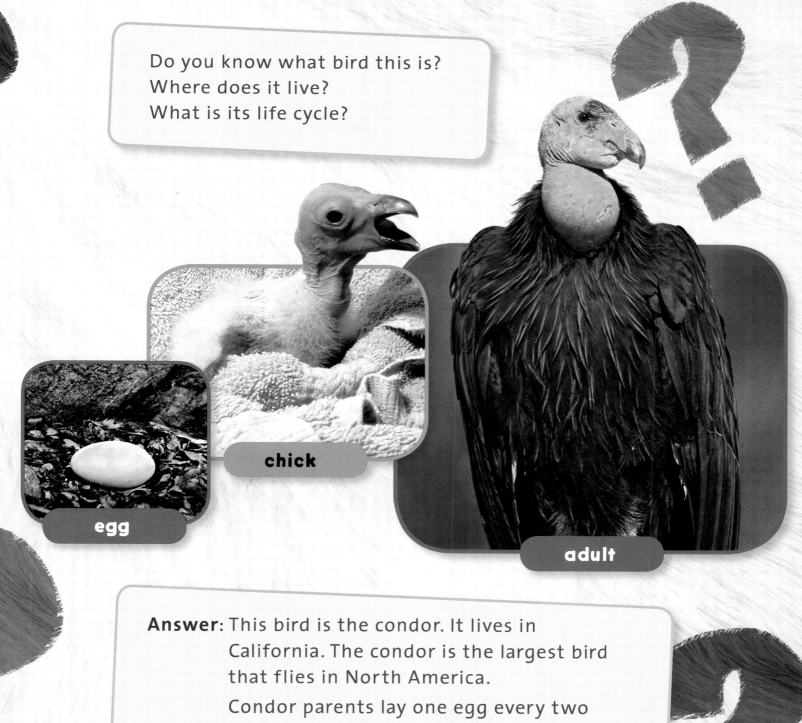

Do you know what bird this is?
Where does it live?
What is its life cycle?

egg

chick

adult

Answer: This bird is the condor. It lives in California. The condor is the largest bird that flies in North America.

Condor parents lay one egg every two years. When the egg hatches, the parents take care of the chick for up to a year. When the chick is an adult, it will have black feathers like those of its parents.

life cycles are different for different animals, such as butterflies, frogs, and mice; **SCI2c** Students know many characteristics of an organism are inherited from the parents. Some characteristics are caused or influenced by the environment.

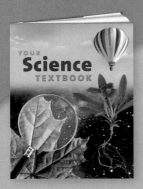

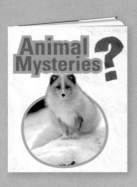

Comparing Texts

I. How is the information in this lesson's three selections alike? How is it different?

2. In what way is the condor family in "Animal Mysteries" like the dog family in "Following Lab Directions"?

3. In what ways have you changed as you have grown?

✏ **WRITE** Compare two of your favorite selections. Tell what you liked about each one. Explain how the information was the same.

CALIFORNIA STANDARDS
ENGLISH-LANGUAGE ARTS STANDARDS—Reading 2.5 Restate facts and details in the text to clarify and organize ideas; *Also* **Writing 1.1** Group related ideas and maintain consistent focus.

Content-Area Vocabulary Review

Comparing Words

Choose two words from the red box that are alike in some way. Then complete this sentence to tell how the words are alike.

_____ and _____ are alike

because they both _____.

WORDS ABOUT
Animals

life cycle

larva

pupa

environment

Draw It

Choose a word from the red box. Write it on the back of a sheet of paper. On the front, draw a picture about your word. Ask your partner to guess the word by looking at the picture. Then use other vocabulary words to tell about your picture.

Mapping Our

Reading and labeling maps helps us understand our world. We can see communities both near and far away.

In this lesson, you will read

- "Land and Water"
- "How to Label a Map of North America"
- "How California Land Is Used"

World

Content-Area Vocabulary

R1.8
H-SS2.2.2

WORDS ABOUT
Geography

continents

landform

directional
  indicator

bodies of water

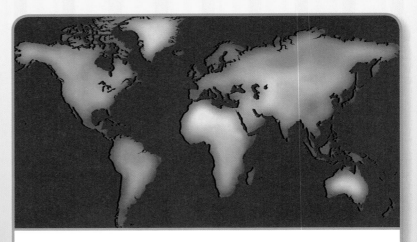

There are seven continents on Earth. A **continent** is a very large area of land, such as North America, that is made up of one or more countries.

A mountain is one kind of landform. A **landform** is land with a special feature or shape, such as a hill, mountain, or valley.

CALIFORNIA STANDARDS
ENGLISH-LANGUAGE ARTS STANDARDS—Reading 1.8 Use knowledge of individual words in unknown compound words to predict their meaning. *Also* **History-Social Science 2.2.2** Label from memory a simple map of North American continent, including the countries, oceans, Great Lakes, major rivers, and mountain ranges. Identify the essential map elements: title, legend, directional indicator, scale, and date.

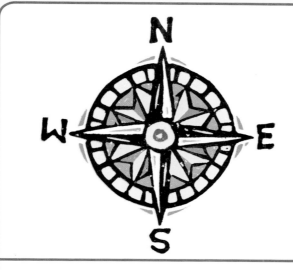

This directional indicator shows the four main points of direction. A **directional indicator** on a map shows the directions north, south, east, and west.

This ocean is a large body of water. A **body of water** is a certain size and shape of water on Earth, such as a lake, river, or ocean.

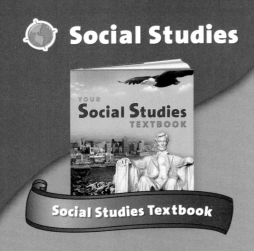

Social Studies Textbook

Read to

- learn about and locate countries in North America.
- tell about land forms and bodies of water.
- locate a directional indicator on a map.

R2.5
HSS2.2
HSS2.2.2

Land and Water

Did you ever think about how the surface of Earth is made up of land and water? Let's learn about the land.

The biggest areas of land are called **continents.** There are seven continents in all. We live on the continent of North America.

North America

Most continents have many countries. A **country** is an area of land with its own people and laws. North America has three big countries. The United States, where we live, is one of them. The other two big countries are its neighbors—Canada, to the north, and Mexico, to the south.

North America also has many small countries. These countries are in the southern part of the continent, in Central America.

Question On which continent is the United States?

CALIFORNIA STANDARDS
ENGLISH-LANGUAGE ARTS STANDARDS—Reading 2.5 Restate facts and details in the text to clarify and organize ideas; *Also* History-Social Science 2.2 Students demonstrate map skills by describing the absolute and relative locations of people, places, and environments; **HSS2.2.2** Label from memory a simple map of the North American continent, including the countries, oceans, Great Lakes, major rivers, and mountain ranges. Identify the essential map elements: title, legend, directional indicator, scale, and date.

The United States is a large country in
North America.

Landforms

North America has many different landforms. A **landform** is land with a special shape or feature.

One kind of landform is a plain, which is flat land. Plains are found in the middle section of North America in both the United States and Canada. Some plains in our country are called the Great Plains.

hills

plains

North America also has many hills. A **hill** is land that rises above the land around it.

A mountain is a high hill. Some mountains always have snow on their peaks, which are the tops of mountains.

Sometimes mountains are close together. They make up a mountain range. North America has several mountain ranges that stretch across parts of the United States. One of these mountain ranges is called the Rocky Mountains. Use the map legend below to help you find it.

Question **What are some kinds of landforms?**

Land of North America

ARCTIC OCEAN

North
West — East
South

PACIFIC OCEAN

ROCKY MOUNTAINS

GREAT PLAINS

Mississippi River

Hudson Bay

Great Lakes

APPALACHIAN MTS.

ATLANTIC OCEAN

Gulf of Mexico

Caribbean Sea

0   500   1,000 Miles
0   500 1,000 Kilometers

Legend
Desert
Hills
^^^ Mountains
Plains
Water

mountains

85

Bodies of Water

Many parts of Earth's surface are covered with water. These parts are called **bodies of water**. Bodies of water can be found all over the world. Continents have bodies of water within them.

The biggest bodies of water are oceans. North America lies between two of them: the Atlantic Ocean and the Pacific Ocean.

Question Between which two oceans can you find North America?

Land and Water of North America

ARCTIC OCEAN

GREENLAND

Bering Sea

North
West — East
South

PACIFIC OCEAN

Hudson Bay

ROCKY MOUNTAINS

GREAT PLAINS

Mississippi River

Great Lakes

APPALACHIAN MTS.

ATLANTIC OCEAN

Legend
Desert
Hills
∧∧ Mountains
Plains
Water

Gulf of Mexico

Caribbean Sea

0   500   1,000 Miles
0   500 1,000 Kilometers

The Mississippi River flows from north to south.

A **river** is a large stream of water that flows across the land. Rivers are found throughout North America. The Mississippi River is a large river in the United States. It flows from near the northern border of Canada south to another body of water, the Gulf of Mexico.

A **lake** is also a body of water. It has land all around it. The Great Lakes are located between the United States and Canada. They make up the largest group of freshwater lakes in the world. Can you find them on the map?

Question   Why are the Great Lakes special?

Reading Maps

You can read maps to find out where continents, countries, mountains, oceans, and other landforms are located. The main directions are north, south, east, and west. These four main directions are called **cardinal directions**.

Look at the map below. Find the symbol that shows the cardinal directions. This is called a directional indicator.

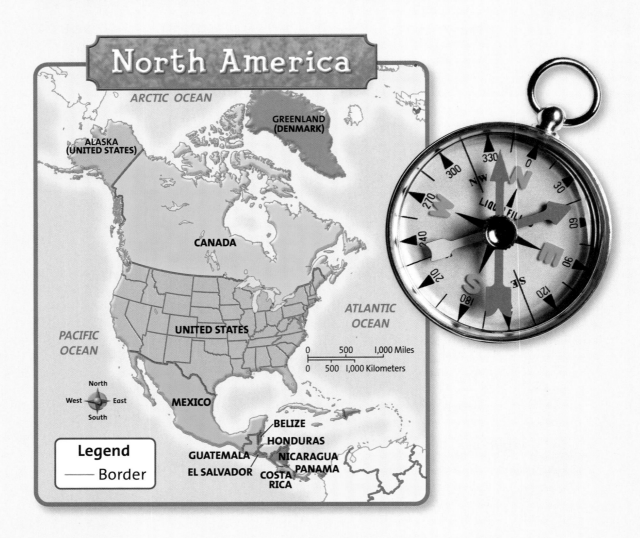

North America

ARCTIC OCEAN

GREENLAND
(DENMARK)

ALASKA
(UNITED STATES)

CANADA

PACIFIC
OCEAN

UNITED STATES

ATLANTIC
OCEAN

0   500   1,000 Miles
0   500   1,000 Kilometers

North
West ✦ East
South

MEXICO

BELIZE

HONDURAS

GUATEMALA   NICARAGUA
EL SALVADOR   COSTA   PANAMA
              RICA

Legend
—— Border

What country is the southern neighbor of the United States? Use the directional indicator to find south. Mexico is our neighbor to the south.

Pretend that you want to go from the Pacific Ocean to the Atlantic Ocean. In which direction will you travel? Look at the map and find the oceans. Use the directional indicator to find the direction to travel. To get to the Atlantic Ocean from the Pacific Ocean, you would travel east.

Think and Respond

R2.5
HSS2.2

1. What are the three big countries in North America? IMPORTANT DETAILS

R2.5
HSS2.2

2. What kind of landforms can be found on North America? What bodies of water are in or near North America? IMPORTANT DETAILS

R2.5
HSS2.2
HSS2.2.2

3. Point to the directional indicator on the map on page 86. Use it to tell which direction you would go to travel from California to the Mississippi River. GRAPHIC AIDS

CALIFORNIA STANDARDS
ENGLISH-LANGUAGE ARTS STANDARDS—Reading 2.5 Restate facts and details in the text to clarify and organize ideas. *Also* **History-Social Science 2.2** Students demonstrate map skills by describing the absolute and relative locations of people, places, and environments. **HSS2.2.2** Label from memory a simple map of the North American continent, including the countries, oceans, Great Lakes, major rivers, and mountain ranges. Identify the essential map elements: title, legend, directional indicator, scale, and date.

89

R2.5
HSS2.2.2

How to Label a Map of North America

by Alys Thomas

Suppose you have a blank map of North America to label. How will you make sure that you do not miss anything? Think about the parts of the map.

First, give your map a title. Next, think about the countries shown on the map. Work down from the top. Label Canada, the United States of America, and Mexico.

Then, think about the bodies of water. Label the Pacific Ocean to the west and the Atlantic Ocean to the east. The Great Lakes are between Canada and the United States. They will be near the middle of the map. Label them, too.

Now, label the Mississippi River. It runs north to south through the United States.

CALIFORNIA STANDARDS
ENGLISH-LANGUAGE ARTS STANDARDS—Reading 2.5 Restate facts and details in the text to clarify and organize ideas. *Also* **History-Social Science 2.2.2** Label from memory a simple map of the North American continent, including the countries, oceans, Great Lakes, major rivers, and mountain ranges. Identify the essential map elements: title, legend, directional indicator, scale, and date.

Then, look for the mountain symbol. The Rocky Mountains are on the western side of North America. The Appalachian Mountains are on the eastern side of the United States. Label both mountain ranges.

Finally, go back and check that you have labeled countries, oceans, lakes, rivers, and mountains. If you know more features, go ahead and label them. You might even get extra credit!

Map of _____

Legend
^^^ Mountains

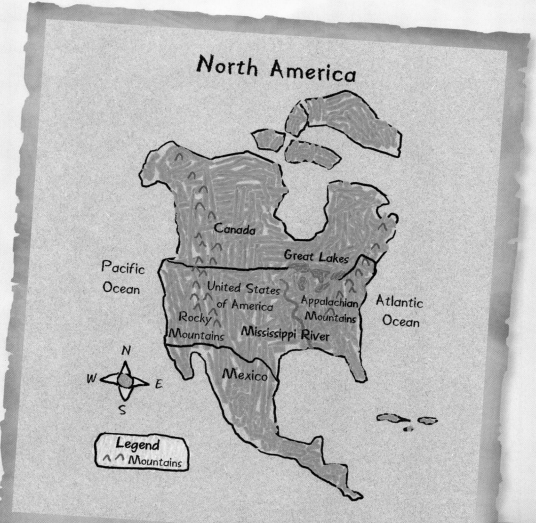

North America

Canada

Great Lakes

Pacific Ocean

United States of America

Appalachian Mountains

Atlantic Ocean

Rocky Mountains

Mississippi River

Mexico

N
W — E
S

Legend
^ ^ Mountains

Nonfiction

R2.3
HSS2.2.4

How California Land Is Used

by Mike Graf

Do you know that more than 36 million people live in California? Many people live in or near cities. Los Angeles, San Diego, and San Francisco are the biggest cities. They are along the coast. The weather is warmer there in the winter. It is cooler in the summer.

Greetings from San Francisco

A postcard scene of San Francisco

CALIFORNIA STANDARDS
ENGLISH-LANGUAGE ARTS STANDARDS—Reading 2.3 Use knowledge of the author's purpose(s) to comprehend informational text. *Also* **History-Social Science 2.2.4** Compare and contrast basic land use in urban, suburban, and rural environments in California.

This map shows some of California's largest cities. It also shows different land areas.

Map of California

Legend
- Coast
- Mountains
- Central Valley
- Desert

OREGON

IDAHO

NEVADA

ARIZONA

MEXICO

PACIFIC OCEAN

Central Valley

Sacramento River

Sierra Nevada

Lake Tahoe

Sacramento ★

San Francisco

San Joaquin River

Central Valley

Yosemite National Park

Fresno

Death Valley

Mojave Desert

North
West — East
South

0   100   200 Miles
0   100   200 Kilometers

Los Angeles

Salton Sea

Imperial Valley

San Diego

The Central Valley of California has many farms and ranches. This 400-mile-long valley is nicknamed the "fruit basket of the world." One fourth of all of America's food is grown here. Grapes, almonds, cotton, and rice are some of the crops. Some grapes are dried for raisins.

Scenes from the Central Valley

Visit the California Vineyards.

Experience the San Joaquin Valley Rice Fields.

Visit Palm Springs.

Greetings from Santa Clarita

Come and See Death Valley.

Scenes from southern California

Much of southern California is desert. Death
Valley is a famous dry place in this area.

The mountains of the Sierra Nevada are cold and snowy in the winter. This part of the state has fewer cities and farms.

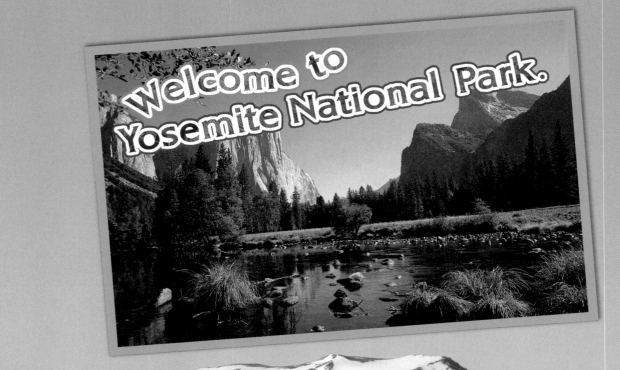

Welcome to Yosemite National Park.

Cattle grazing near the Sierra Nevada

In the north, some places get a lot of rain. Many mountain areas are also very wet. Winter rains and snow fill California's lakes.

California's stored water is used in summer when it doesn't rain. This stored water is moved to drier areas.

The Imperial Valley is in the far south. It gets water this way. Los Angeles also gets some of its water this way.

What is the land like where you live? How is it used?

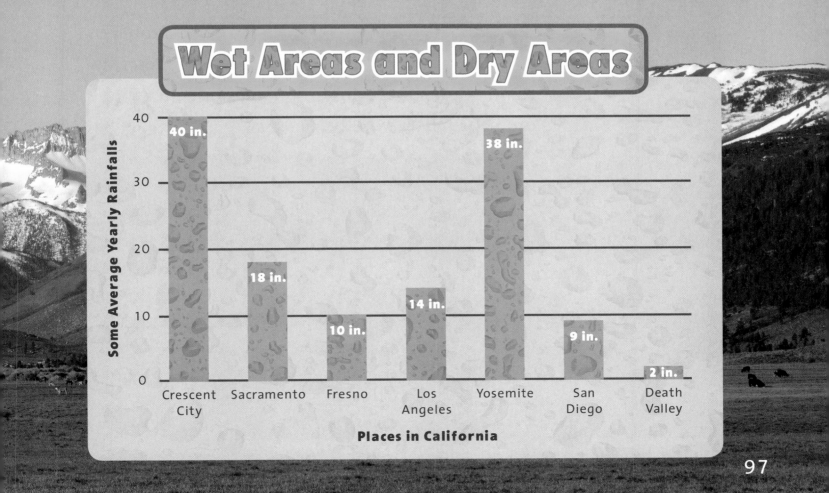

Wet Areas and Dry Areas

Some Average Yearly Rainfalls

- Crescent City: 40 in.
- Sacramento: 18 in.
- Fresno: 10 in.
- Los Angeles: 14 in.
- Yosemite: 38 in.
- San Diego: 9 in.
- Death Valley: 2 in.

Places in California

Comparing Texts

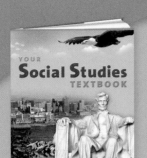

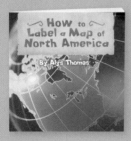

1. What information from "Land and Water" and "How California Land Is Used" would you need to know to label a map of North America?

2. How is land used in the area where you live?

3. Why is it important for people to know how to use a map?

🖊 **WRITE** Use details from "Land and Water" and "How California Land Is Used" to describe some of the landforms and bodies of water that are near where you live.

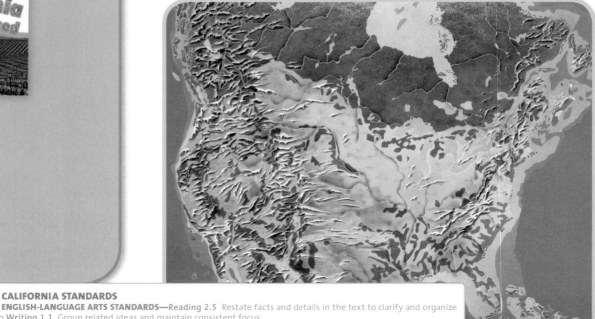

CALIFORNIA STANDARDS
ENGLISH-LANGUAGE ARTS STANDARDS—Reading 2.5 Restate facts and details in the text to clarify and organize ideas. *Also* **Writing 1.1** Group related ideas and maintain consistent focus.

Content-Area Vocabulary Review

Give a Clue

Write the Vocabulary Words on slips of paper. Place the slips face down. With a partner, take turns choosing a slip of paper. On your turn, look at the Vocabulary Word on the paper and give your partner clues about the word. Without saying the Vocabulary Word, try to get your partner to guess what it is.

WORDS ABOUT Geography

continents

landform

directional indicator

bodies of water

Classifying Words

Think of two groups into which you could sort the Vocabulary Words. Draw a chart like the one below, and write each group's name at the top of a column. Then sort the words and write each one in the correct column on the chart. Discuss with your partner why you sorted the words the way you did.

Moving

From helping nature to building communities, we must plan and work together. Then even small projects can bring big results.

In this lesson, you will read

- "The Giant Cabbage"
- "A Tale of Two Mice"
- "The Ant and the Grasshopper"
- "From Seed to Pumpkin"

Forward

Content-Area Vocabulary

R1.6
SCI2e

WORDS ABOUT
Plant Life Cycles

shoots

pollen

energy

kernel

These shoots push through the soil. Plants that are beginning to grow are called **shoots**.

These daisies have lots of pollen. **Pollen** is a powder made by flowers.

 CALIFORNIA STANDARDS
ENGLISH-LANGUAGE ARTS STANDARDS—Reading 1.6 Read aloud fluently and accurately with appropriate intonation and expression. **SCI2e** Students know light, gravity, touch, or environmental stress can affect the germination, growth, and development of plants.

Green plants use energy from the sun to help them grow. **Energy** is the power from a source that makes things work or move.

These are a few kernels of corn. A **kernel** of something is one small part of it.

Folktale

The GIANT Cabbage
An Alaska Folktale

by Cherie B. Stihler

illustrated by Jeremiah Trammell

Moose looked out at his wonderful garden. He had rows and rows of tasty vegetables. "The fair starts this week. I need to find my best cabbage for the **Giant** Cabbage Contest." The vegetables had all grown very **large** under the Midnight Sun.

CALIFORNIA STANDARDS
ENGLISH-LANGUAGE ARTS STANDARDS—Reading 2.5 Restate facts and details in the text to clarify and organize ideas. *Also* **Science 1c** Students know the way to change how something is moving is by giving it a push or pull. The size of the change is related to the strength, or the amount of force, of the push or pull. **SCI1d** Students know tools and machines are used to apply pushes and pulls (forces) to make things move.

Then he saw it. It was a **big** cabbage. It was a really **big** cabbage. It was the **biggest** cabbage he had ever seen. "It's **huge!** It's **enormous!**" Moose marveled. "Why, this is a **GIANT** cabbage. This is sure to win a prize at the fair!"

Moose trimmed the cabbage from the plant, and tried to lift the cabbage and load it onto the truck. He pushed and he tugged. He bumped and he shoved, but the cabbage did not move. It did not even budge.

Just then Bear waved hello as she pedaled home from the library. "Please come help me load this cabbage," yelled Moose. Bear came right over. She saw the cabbage. It was a **big** cabbage. It was a really **big** cabbage. It was the **biggest** cabbage she had ever seen.

"It's **huge!** It's **enormous!**" Bear growled.
"Why, this is a **GIANT** cabbage! This is sure to
win a prize at the fair!"

"I cannot lift this cabbage alone," said Moose.

"I will help you," promised Bear. Moose grabbed
hold of the cabbage, and Bear grabbed hold of the
cabbage. They pushed and they tugged, and they
bumped and they shoved, but the cabbage did not
move. It did not even budge.

Wolf trotted by Moose's garden on his way to the post office and saw the cabbage. It was a **big** cabbage. It was a really **big** cabbage. It was the **biggest** cabbage he had ever seen. "It's **huge!** It's **enormous!**" Wolf howled. "Why, this is a **GIANT** cabbage! This is sure to win a prize at the fair!"

"We cannot lift this cabbage alone," said Moose.

"I will help you," promised Wolf.

They all pushed and they tugged. They bumped and they shoved, but the cabbage did not move. It did not even budge.

Fox and Hare jogged down the lane. They stopped when they saw Moose, Bear, and Wolf sitting in Moose's garden. Fox and Hare went over in hopes of a glass of lemonade, but then Fox and Hare saw the cabbage. It was a **big** cabbage. It was a really **big** cabbage. It was the **biggest** cabbage they had ever seen. "It's **huge!** It's **enormous!**" barked Fox.

"Why, this is a **GIANT** cabbage! This is sure to win a prize at the fair!" said Hare, hopping up and down.

"We cannot lift this cabbage alone," said Moose.

"We will help you," promised Fox and Hare. They all pushed and they tugged. They bumped and they shoved, but the cabbage did not move. It did not even budge.

Old Porcupine waddled along then. She saw her friends sitting in the middle of Moose's garden. Old Porcupine's eyes were not as sharp as they used to be, but she soon saw the cabbage. It was a **big** cabbage. It was a really **big** cabbage. It was almost the **biggest** cabbage her old eyes had ever seen.

"Say, that's a pretty **big** cabbage there. That **GIANT** cabbage could win a prize at the fair!" Porcupine said.

"We cannot lift this cabbage alone," complained Moose.

"I will help you," promised Old Porcupine, "but first, we need some tools." Old Porcupine sent Wolf to find her toolbox. Bear and Fox found wood for a ramp, and Moose found a rope in his garden shed. Hare moved the truck closer. At last they were ready to try again.

Old Porcupine grabbed hold of the ends of the rope. The others pushed and they tugged. They bumped and they shoved, and the cabbage began to move, but only a budge.

Squirrel scampered down from his tree to see what all the fuss was about. He saw the cabbage. It was a **big** cabbage. It was a really **big** cabbage. It was the **biggest** cabbage he had ever seen. "It's **huge!** It's **enormous!**" Squirrel chattered. "Why, this is a **GIANT** cabbage! This is sure to win a prize at the fair!"

"Well, it might," Bear sighed, "but we have not been able to lift this cabbage."

"Have you tried a stick?" suggested Squirrel. "I use sticks to move rocks that cover my cache of nuts." The animal friends thought this was a splendid idea.

"This may be just the thing we need to load this cabbage onto the truck," said Wolf, pulling over a strong branch. Moose, Bear, Wolf, Fox and Hare grabbed hold of the cabbage. Old Porcupine grabbed hold of the ends of the rope, and Squirrel grabbed hold of the branch.

They pushed and they tugged. They bumped and they shoved, and the cabbage began to move . . . but only another budge.

"What we need is just a teeny, tiny, little more of a push," insisted Old Porcupine.

"We're tired! We can't push any harder," whined Fox, but the animal friends would not give up. So they sat and they rested.

As the Midnight Sun moved across the sky,
Little Vole poked her nose out of her burrow. She
saw the cabbage. It was a big cabbage. It was a
really big cabbage. It was the biggest cabbage
she had ever seen. "It's huge! It's enormous!"
Vole squeaked. "Why, this is a GIANT cabbage!
This is sure to win a prize at the fair!"

"Well, it might," Moose said, "but we cannot lift
this cabbage."

"I will help you," promised Little Vole.

Moose, Bear, Wolf, Fox and Hare grabbed hold of the cabbage. Old Porcupine grabbed hold of the ends of the rope. Squirrel grabbed hold of the branch, and Little Vole grabbed hold of the last, teeny, tiny, little open spot on the cabbage's side.

They pushed and they tugged. They bumped and they shoved. Then they all pushed a little bit more, and the cabbage began to move up the ramp ever so slowly, until . . .

KEEEEEEEEEEEERWHUMP!

The **GIANT** cabbage landed with a thump and
a bumpity-bump.

"HOORAY!" shouted the animals. Then they
sat down with a thump and a bumpity-bump.

"We did it!" panted Hare.

"Oh, thank you, my dear, dear friends!" cried
Moose. "Now we can go to the fair!" The animal
friends scrambled into the truck and thumped and
bumped down the road to the fair.

At the fair, the **GIANT** cabbage rolled slowly back down the ramp and landed with a thump and a bumpity-bump right in front of the judges. The judges looked surprised. It was a **big** cabbage. It was a really **big** cabbage. It was the **biggest** cabbage they had ever seen. "It's **huge!** It's **enormous!**" they marveled. "Why, this **GIANT** cabbage wins the prize for the fair!"

"**HOORAY!**" shouted the animals again. "Let's go have fun at the fair!"

"Now we need to get all this fine cabbage home for our supper," said Moose.

"It's a good thing I brought Old Porcupine's tool box," said Wolf. Soon, the **GIANT** cabbage was trimmed into a **GIANT** pile of cabbage pieces. Moose and Bear grabbed hold of the extra-large pieces of cabbage. Wolf and Fox grabbed hold of the large pieces of cabbage. Hare and Old Porcupine grabbed hold of the medium pieces of cabbage. Squirrel grabbed hold of a small piece of cabbage, and Little Vole grabbed the last teeny, tiny, little piece of cabbage.

They pushed and they tugged. They bumped and they shoved, and they plopped the **GIANT** cabbage pieces into the back of the truck. Then Moose, Bear, Wolf, Fox and Hare, Old Porcupine, Squirrel, and Little Vole scrambled into the truck— and they thumped and bumped back down the road to Moose's house.

"Let's make some cabbage soup," suggested Moose. The animal friends ran home. Then they pushed and they tugged, they bumped and they shoved, and they brought things for the soup. Moose dropped in the cabbage and stirred the pot. Bear dropped in potatoes and stirred the pot. Wolf dropped in squash and stirred the pot.

Fox and Hare dropped in onions and carrots and stirred the pot. Old Porcupine brought loaves of her freshly baked bread. Squirrel dropped in spices and stirred the pot one more time, and the dinner was complete with a yummy berry treat made by their own Little Vole.

The animals danced and sang while the giant soup pot bubbled. Then they ate a wonderful meal of Moose's **GIANT**, and now prize-winning cabbage as they celebrated their friendship under the Midnight Sun.

(There are still probably leftovers if you really want some!)

Friends and family who work together can get any job done—and sometimes it's the tiniest of friends who make things happen. This is part of the spirit of Alaska.

Think and Respond

 1. In the beginning, how did the animals try to move the cabbage? IMPORTANT DETAILS

 2. Why did Moose think that having more animals push and pull the cabbage might make it easier to move? DRAW CONCLUSIONS

 3. How did the animals use tools to help them move the cabbage onto the truck? IMPORTANT DETAILS

CALIFORNIA STANDARDS
ENGLISH-LANGUAGE ARTS STANDARDS—Reading 2.5 Restate facts and details in the text to clarify and organize ideas. *Also*
Science 1c Students know the way to change how something is moving is by giving it a push or pull. The size of the change is related to the strength, or the amount of force, of the push or pull. **SCI1d** Students know tools and machines are used to apply pushes and pulls (forces) to make things move.

Two Fables

R3.3
HSS2.4.3

A Tale of Two Mice

A Sioux Fable retold by Ermine May
illustrated by Miguel Tanco

Early one morning Busy Mouse sniffed the crisp fall air. She scurried along and saw that the grass had turned brown. "Oh, my," she said. "It is time to begin collecting seeds. I will need enough to last until spring."

CALIFORNIA STANDARDS
ENGLISH-LANGUAGE ARTS STANDARDS—Reading 3.3 Compare and contrast different versions of the same stories that reflect different cultures; *Also* **History-Social Science 2.4.3** Understand how limits on resources affect production and consumption (what to produce and what to consume).

A few moons later, a different little mouse, a more playful mouse, noticed that the sounds of the wolf-howl seemed closer. This meant it would be winter soon, since sounds carry better through the late fall air. As Playful Mouse danced all night around the warm campfire, she thought, "I really must begin collecting seeds tomorrow."

The next day, Playful Mouse found Busy Mouse pulling a snakeskin. It was full of seeds. Busy Mouse was taking the seeds home to her den. She would store them for winter. Playful Mouse asked her, "What shall I do? I don't have any seeds."

Busy Mouse told Playful Mouse, "I have an extra snakeskin that I found one night. I will let you use it. You must begin collecting seeds today!"

Playful Mouse took the snakeskin but never filled it. Soon, a blanket of snow fell across the prairie. All winter long Playful Mouse was cold and hungry while Busy Mouse was fat and happy in her den.

Moral: Do not put off until tomorrow what you should do today.

The Ant and the Grasshopper

An Aesop Fable retold by Ann McGovern

One fine summer's day, a Grasshopper was chirping and singing as if he had not a care in the world. An Ant passed by, struggling with a kernel of corn which he was carrying to his nest. The Grasshopper called to the busy Ant, "Come and visit with me for a while. It is far too nice a day to be working."

The Ant looked at the Grasshopper. "I observe you do nothing but sing all day," he said. "I do not have time to sing and play. I am storing up food for the long winter days ahead, and I suggest you do the same." The Grasshopper laughed and said, "Why worry about winter? I have enough food for the present."

Months passed. The snow lay on the fields. The Ant was content. In his house there was food to last all winter. The Grasshopper had nothing to eat. "Ah," he said sadly, "I am dying of hunger. If only I had realized that it is best to prepare today for the needs of tomorrow."

129

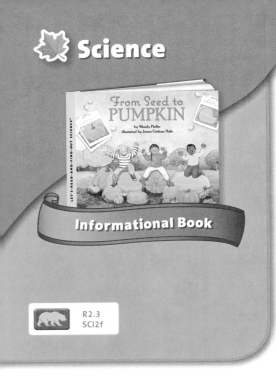

Informational Book

R2.3
SCI2f

From Seed to Pumpkin

by Wendy Pfeffer
illustrated by James Graham Hale

When spring winds warm the earth, a farmer plants hundreds of pumpkin seeds. Every pumpkin seed can become a baby pumpkin plant. Underground, covered with dark, moist soil, the baby plants begin to grow. As the plants get bigger, the seeds crack open. Stems sprout up. Roots dig down. Inside the roots are tubes. Water travels up these tubes the way juice goes up a straw.

CALIFORNIA STANDARDS
ENGLISH-LANGUAGE ARTS STANDARDS—Reading 2.3 Use knowledge of the author's purpose(s) to comprehend informational text. *Also* **Science 2f** Students know flowers and fruits are associated with reproduction in plants.

In less than two weeks from planting time, green shoots poke up through the earth. These shoots grow into tiny seedlings. Two leaves, called seed leaves, uncurl on each stem. They reach up toward the sun. Sunlight gives these leaves energy to make food.

Like us, plants need food to grow. Green plants do not eat food as we do. Their leaves make it. To make food, plants need light, water, and air. Leaves catch the sunlight. Roots soak up rainwater. Little openings in the leaves let air in. Using energy from the sun, the leaves mix the air with water from the soil to make sugar. This feeds the plant.

Soon broad, prickly leaves with jagged edges unfold on the stems. The seed leaves dry up. Now the new leaves make food for the pumpkin plant. Each pumpkin stem has many sets of tubes. One tube in each set takes water from the soil up to the leaves so they can make sugar. The other tube in each set sends food back down so the pumpkin can grow.

The days grow warmer. The farmer tends the pumpkin patch to keep weeds out. Weeds take water from the soil. Pumpkin plants need that water to grow.

Pumpkin plants don't stand up tall. As the stems grow longer, they sprawl all over the ground. Before long, twisted, tangled vines cover the pumpkin patch.

Soon flower buds appear on the vines. After each bud opens, its orange petals grow bigger and bigger. They look like bright orange umbrellas. During the heat of the day, the flowers close. They open again during the cool nights and early mornings.

The bright orange flowers attract swarms of bees. The bees buzz about, carrying yellow pollen from the male flowers to the female flowers. Now pumpkins can grow. The petals wither away. Where the flowers bloomed, tiny hard fruits begin to grow. Hundreds of these cling to the vines.

The days grow hot. All summer the warm sun and the cool rain help the tiny fruits grow larger and larger. Soon summer is over. The cornstalks next to the pumpkin patch turn brown. Leaves on trees turn red, orange, and yellow. Pumpkins change color, too. As they ripen, they change from green to yellow, then to orange.

In just four months small, flat, white pumpkin seeds have grown into big, fat, orange pumpkins. The pumpkins are ripe and round, with lumps and bumps. They come in all sizes and shapes. They're waiting in the autumn sun.

135

Science

Social Studies

Comparing Texts

R2.5
W1.1
SCI2.a

1. How are Busy Mouse from "A Tale of Two Mice" and the Ant from "The Ant and the Grasshopper" the same?

2. What lesson can you learn from "The Giant Cabbage"?

3. Why is it important for people to work together?

✏ **WRITE** How does a seed become a plant? Use information in "From Seed to Pumpkin" to help you explain.

Content-Area Vocabulary Review

Comparing Words

Choose two Vocabulary Words that are alike in some way. Finish the sentence below to tell how the words are alike.

_____ and _____ are alike

because they both _____.

Classifying Words

Think of two groups into which you could sort the Vocabulary Words. Draw a chart like the one below, and write each group's name at the top of a column. Then sort the words and write each one in the correct column on the chart. Discuss with your partner why you sorted the words the way you did.

Tracing Our

There are many ways to find and share information about your family history. You can also find out about the world around you.

In this lesson, you will read

- "Grandma Lai Goon Remembers"
- "How to Make a Time Line"
- "Using a Map Grid"

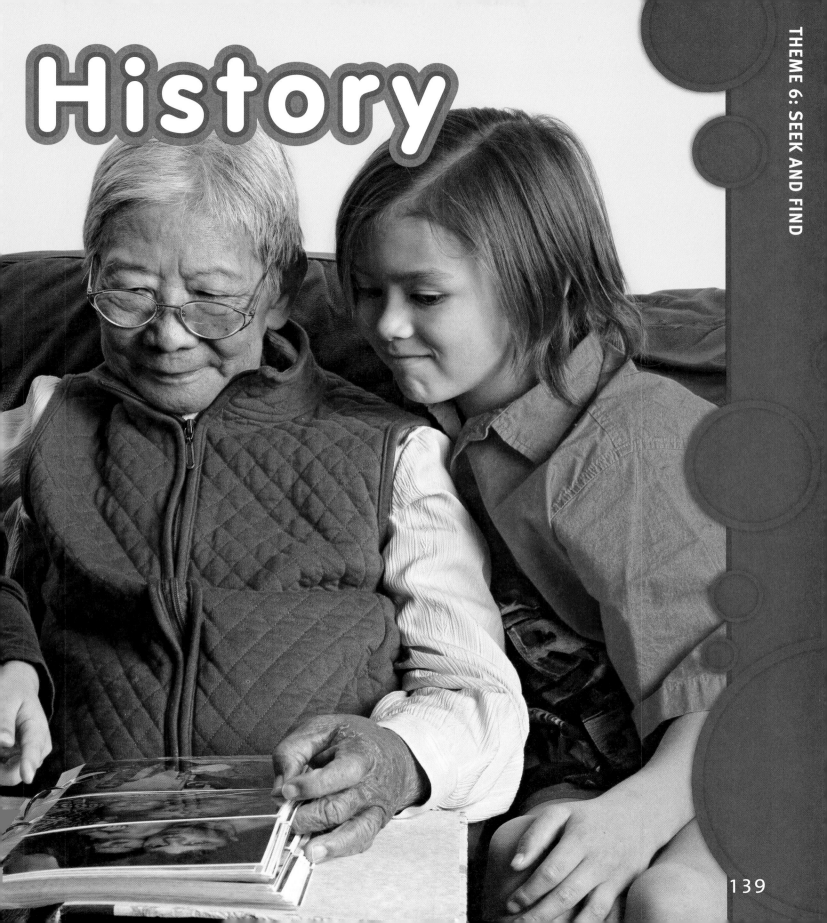

History

Content-Area Vocabulary

H-SS2.1.2

WORDS ABOUT
World Culture
and History

tai chi

calligraphy

interview

family tree

These people are doing tai chi. When someone does **tai chi,** he or she is doing special Chinese exercises to make the mind and body stronger.

This kind of writing is called calligraphy. **Calligraphy** is the art of beautiful handwriting made by using a special pen or brush.

CALIFORNIA STANDARDS
History-Social Science 2.1.2 Compare and contrast their daily lives with those of their parents, grandparents, and/or guardians.

The woman on the left is at an interview for a job. An **interview** is a meeting in which someone asks another person questions to get information.

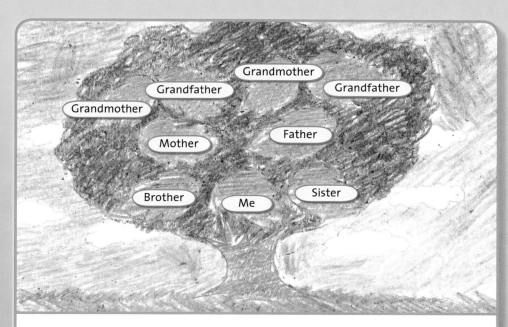

I have a large family tree. A **family tree** is a chart that shows all the people in a family over many years.

GRANDMA LAI GOON REMEMBERS

Nonfiction

Read to

- compare and contrast modern daily life with that of the past.

- learn about the history of a family through primary sources.

- learn ways to find out about your own family history.

R2.5
HSS2.1.1
HSS2.1.2

GRANDMA LAI GOON REMEMBERS

A Chinese-American Family Story

by Ann Morris
photographs and illustrations
by Peter Linenthal

"Well, how was school today?" Grandma Lai Goon asks as she meets Allyson and Daniel at the bus stop.

"Great," reply the children. Excitedly they tell their grandmother about their day at school. Daniel shows her a project he has been working on.

Allyson, age eight, and Daniel, age nine, greet Grandma Lai Goon.

CALIFORNIA STANDARDS
ENGLISH-LANGUAGE ARTS STANDARDS—Reading 2.5 Restate facts and details in the text to clarify and organize ideas; *Also*
History-Social Science 2.1.1 Trace the history of a family through the use of primary and secondary sources, including artifacts, photographs, interviews, and documents; **HSS2.1.2** Compare and contrast their daily lives with those of their parents, grandparents, and/ or guardians.

Allyson and Daniel live with their older sister, Sarah, and their parents in an apartment near San Francisco's Chinatown. Mary and Wilson, their parents, work all day in the city as social workers, helping people solve problems. Grandma Lai Goon takes care of Allyson and Daniel before and after school.

143

Grandma Lai Goon lives in an apartment around the corner from the children and their parents. She has lived there for many years. It is the same apartment that Mary grew up in. Besides Mary, Lai Goon has two daughters and one son. Mary was the youngest.

In Chinese, "Lai" means beautiful. The children call Lai Goon "Paw Paw," which means grandmother.

Allyson and Daniel enjoy spending time with Grandma Lai Goon. Sometimes she shows them her family album. As they look through the old family photographs together, she tells them stories about her life.

Lai Goon doesn't speak English. She speaks to the children in Chinese, the language she learned when she was growing up.

Grandma Lai Goon was born in Dic Hoy, a small village in Canton, China, more than seventy years ago. There were six people in Grandma Lai Goon's family—Lai Goon, her father and mother, two brothers, and one sister.

"My father was very strict," Lai Goon tells Allyson and Daniel. "He expected us to have good manners. He always reminded us to say good morning to our elders before going out to play or work."

She also remembers that he was very kind. "He always took good care of me when I was sick," she says, "and gave me medicines made from herbs and plants."

Traditional Chinese herbs

When Grandma Lai Goon was nineteen, she left Dic Hoy to find work in another town. Before long she met a young man, Chuck Woon, and they got married. Soon after, Chuck Woon left China to find work in San Francisco. In 1949 Lai Goon joined him. She got a job in a sewing factory and began to raise a family. Even though she and Chuck Woon didn't have much money, they made sure that their children went to college.

Lai Goon is retired now, but she keeps busy. She takes care of Allyson and Daniel. And every morning she does tai chi, Chinese exercises that she learned ten years ago. These movements help strengthen the body and the mind. Many people say that Lai Goon is so good at tai chi that she could be a teacher!

When they come home from school, Grandma Lai Goon often teaches Allyson and Daniel skills she learned when she was growing up. Allyson and Daniel learn to write Chinese words with a special brush and black ink. This kind of writing is called calligraphy.

梁余麗娟

周潤良周寶儀

Daniel

Lai Goon

Allyson

This is Daniel, Allyson, and Lai Goon in Chinese.

Grandma Lai Goon also teaches her grandchildren how to make Chinese dolls.

"This is the way we made the dolls in Dic Hoy," explains Lai Goon. "We used incense sticks for the body," Lai Goon explains. "For heads, we used black clay from the riverbank where I went digging for clams. For hair we used the silky roots of rice plants, and for clothes we sewed together pieces of old cloth."

When Grandma Lai Goon was a girl, she played a pebble game that is something like American jacks. It uses stones instead of jacks and a ball. Allyson and Daniel enjoy playing Chinese "jacks" with Lai Goon, their mother, and their older sister, Sarah.

Grandma Lai Goon is a good cook. Her specialty Chinese buns are called "bow." Sometimes the children help her make bow, tasting bits of it as they cook.

The best part about bow is eating them!
"They are so delicious," says Allyson.
The whole family enjoys Lai Goon's bow.

Allyson, Mary, and Lai Goon

ALL ABOUT MY FAMILY

Would you like to know about your family? Here are some things you can do.

INTERVIEWS

You will find out many interesting things about your relatives by interviewing them. Ask them questions about their childhood—where they lived, what they liked best to do and to eat, what they read and studied in school. Find out, too, how things are different today from when they were young. Use a tape recorder to record your questions and their answers.

FAMILY ALBUM

Ask your relatives for pictures of themselves. Put all the pictures in an album. Write something you have learned about each person under his or her picture.

FAMILY TREE

All of us have many relatives. Some of us are born into the family. Others are related by marriage or have been adopted. You can make a family tree that looks like the one on this page to show who belongs to your family.

Leong Family Tree

Lai Goon

Chuck Woon

Wilson

Mary

Daniel and Allyson

Sarah

Think and Respond

R2.5
HSS2.1.2

1. How are the lives of Daniel and Allyson different from the life of Grandma Lai Goon when she was growing up? How are they the same? COMPARE AND CONTRAST

R2.5
HSS2.1.1

2. How does Grandma Lai Goon share information about her past with Daniel and Allyson? What are some ways that you can learn about your own family history? IMPORTANT DETAILS

R2.5
HSS2.1.2

3. How is your childhood the same as that of a parent or grandparent? How is it different? COMPARE AND CONTRAST

CALIFORNIA STANDARDS
ENGLISH-LANGUAGE ARTS STANDARDS—Reading 2.5 Restate facts and details in the text to clarify and organize ideas; *Also*
History-Social Science 2.1.1 Trace the history of a family through the use of primary and secondary sources, including artifacts, photographs, interviews, and documents; **HSS2.1.2** Compare and contrast their daily lives with those of their parents, grandparents, and/or guardians.

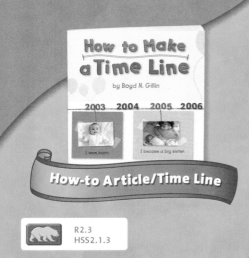

How to Make a Time Line
by Boyd N. Gillin

2003 2004 2005 2006

I was born.

I became a big sister.

How-to Article/Time Line

R2.3
HSS2.1.3

How to Make a Time Line

by Boyd N. Gillin

Biographies tell us about important events in people's lives. Another way to tell about important events is to use a time line. A time line is a line that puts information in order. Read a time line from left to right, just as you would read a sentence on a page.

2003   2004   2005   2006

I was born.

I became a big sister.

CALIFORNIA STANDARDS
ENGLISH-LANGUAGE ARTS STANDARDS—Reading 2.3 Use knowledge of the author's purpose(s) to comprehend informational text. *Also* **History-Social Science 2.1.3** Place important events in their lives in the order in which they occurred.

Here's how to make a time line.

1. Draw a line across the middle of a large sheet of paper, and label it with years. Begin with the year you were born, and end with the year it is now.

2. Write important events in your life on note cards, beginning with your birth. Put the cards in the order that the events happened.

3. Place each note card below the correct year.

4. Glue or tape your note cards to your time line.

5. Draw a line from each card to the correct year. Add photos and other pictures if you like.

2007   2008   2009   2010

I learned to ride my bike.

In second grade I got Beebo, my hamster.

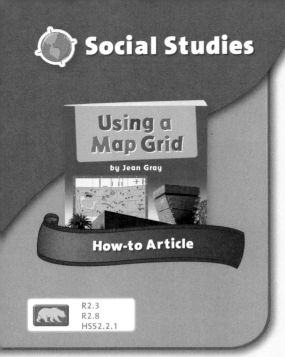

Using a Map Grid
by Jean Gray

How-to Article

R2.3
R2.8
HSS2.2.1

Stow Lake

Using a Map Grid

by Jean Gray

Are you ready to go on a field trip? Pretend that your class is going on a field trip to Golden Gate Park in San Francisco. You will find many interesting places to visit there.

Let's say your teacher gives everyone a map that shows the area of the park that you will be visiting. You see that the map has lines drawn through it. Don't worry. This is a special type of map that uses a map grid.

The lines on a map grid divide the map into squares. The squares are labeled with letters and numbers to help you quickly find a location on the map.

CALIFORNIA STANDARDS
ENGLISH-LANGUAGE ARTS STANDARDS—Reading 2.3 Use knowledge of the author's purpose(s) to comprehend informational text; **R2.8** Follow two-step written instructions. *Also* **History-Social Science 2.2.1** Locate on a simple letter-number grid system the specific locations and geographic features in their neighborhood or community.

Let's see how the map grid works. The first stop on the field trip is the museum.

1. Put your left index finger on the letter B below the top-left corner of the map. Put your right index finger on the number 3 at the top of the map.

2. Bring your left finger across and bring your right finger down until they meet in a square. This is square B-3. Do you see the museum?

Use the map grid to help locate other places in the park.

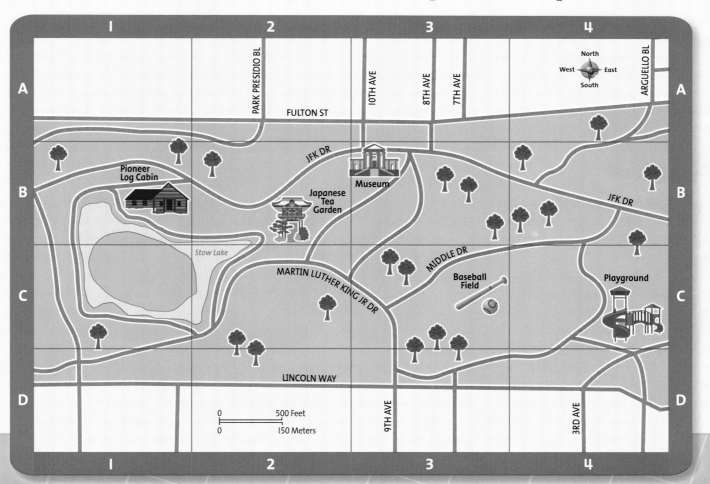

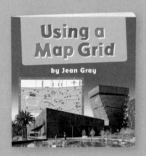

Comparing Texts

I. How can "How to Make a Time Line" help you understand "Grandma Lai Goon Remembers"?

2. How can a map grid help you find a location?

3. Why would making a time line of your life be helpful to others?

✏ **WRITE** What are some ways that families can share what happened long ago?

Leong Family Tree

CALIFORNIA STANDARDS
ENGLISH-LANGUAGE ARTS STANDARDS—Reading 2.5 Restate facts and details in the text to clarify and organize ideas. *Also* **Writing 1.1** Group related ideas and maintain consistent focus.

Content-Area Vocabulary Review

Give a Clue

Write the Vocabulary Words on slips of paper. Place the slips face down. With a partner, take turns choosing a slip of paper.

On your turn, look at the Vocabulary Word on the paper and give your partner clues about the word. Without saying the Vocabulary Word, try to get your partner to guess what it is.

WORDS ABOUT World Culture and History

tai chi

calligraphy

interview

family tree

Draw It

Choose a Vocabulary Word. Write it on the back of a sheet of paper. On the front of the paper, draw a picture about your word. Ask your partner to guess the word by looking at the picture. Then use other Vocabulary Words to tell about your picture.

Using the Glossary

Get to Know It!

The **Glossary** gives the meaning of a word as it is used in the *Student Edition*. It also gives an example sentence that shows how to use the word. The words in the **Glossary** are in ABC order, also called alphabetical order.

Learn to Use It!

If you want to find *energy* in the **Glossary,** you should first find the **E** words. **E** is near the beginning of the alphabet, so the **E** words are near the beginning of the **Glossary.** Then you can use the guide words at the top of the page to help you find the entry word *energy*. It is on page 162.

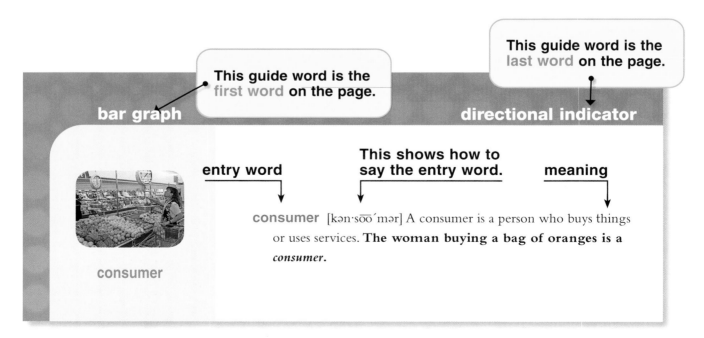

This guide word is the first word on the page.

This guide word is the last word on the page.

bar graph

directional indicator

entry word

This shows how to say the entry word.

meaning

consumer [kən·sŌŌ′mər] A consumer is a person who buys things or uses services. **The woman buying a bag of oranges is a** *consumer.*

consumer

B

bar graph [bär graf] A bar graph is a chart that shows changes in how much there is of something. **The *bar graph* shows how many second graders in a school like chocolate chip cookies.**

bodies of water [bod´ēz uv wôt´ər] A body of water is a certain size and shape of water on Earth, such as a lake, river, or ocean. **An ocean is a large *body of water*.**

bodies of water

C

calligraphy [kə·lig´rə·fē] Calligraphy is the art of creating beautiful handwriting, using a special pen or brush. **There are many kinds of *calligraphy*.**

Congress [kong´gris] Congress is a group of people who make laws for our country. ***Congress* meets in a special building in Washington, D.C.**

consumer [kən·sōō´mər] A consumer is a person who buys things or uses services. **The woman buying a bag of oranges is a *consumer*.**

continents [kon´tə·nənts] A continent is a very large area of land, such as North America, that is made up of one or more countries. **There are seven *continents* on Earth.**

calligraphy

D

directional indicator [di·rek´shən·əl in´də·kāt·ər] A directional indicator on a map shows the directions north, south, east, and west. **The *directional indicator* shows that California is west of Nevada.**

energy

election [i·lek´shən] When people have an election, they vote to choose their leaders. **The children are having an *election* for class president.**

energy [en´ər·jē] Energy is the power from a source that makes things work or move. **Green plants use *energy* from the sun to help make them grow.**

environment [in·vī´rən·mənt] An animal or plant's environment is all the things around it that can help it or make it hard to live, like air, water, and other animals and plants. **The pond is this bird's *environment*.**

 F

family tree [fam´ə·lē trē] A family tree is a chart that shows all the people in a family over many years. **I have a large *family tree*.**

 G

government [guv´ərn·mənt] A government is a group of people who run a community, state, or country. **Our *government* needs good leaders.**

government

 I

interview [in´tər·vyoo] An interview is a meeting in which someone asks another person questions to get information. **He has an *interview* for a job.**

interview

162

K

kernel [kûr´nəl] A kernel of something is one small part of it. **A few *kernels* of corn lay on the ground.**

L

landform [land´fôrm] A landform is land with a special feature or shape, such as a hill, mountain, or valley. **A mountain is one kind of *landform*.**

larva [lär´və] A larva is an early stage of an insect's life when it looks like a short, fat worm. **A caterpillar is the *larva* of a butterfly.**

law [lô] A law is an important rule that people have agreed to follow. ***Laws* help people drive safely.**

life cycle [līf sī´kəl] An animal's life cycle is all the stages and changes it goes through from the time it is born until it dies. **The egg is the first stage in a frog's *life cycle*.**

P

pollen [pol´ən] Pollen is a powder made by flowers that helps new flowers grow. **Bees carry *pollen* from flower to flower.**

pupa [pyōō´pə] A pupa is a stage of insect life between larva and adult, when the insect is in a hard covering and does not move. **A caterpillar becomes a *pupa* and makes a hard covering.**

R

resources [rē´sôrs·əz] The resources of a group of people or a person are materials and other things that they need and use to help them live. **Our natural *resources* are air, land, and water.**

kernels

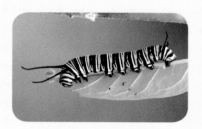

larva

pupa

scarcity

tai chi

scarcity [skâr′sə·tē] If there is a scarcity of something, there is not enough of it for the people who need it or want it. **There is a *scarcity* of water because there is no rain.**

shoots [sho͞ots] Plants that are beginning to grow are called shoots. **The *shoots* push through the soil.**

T

tai chi [tī chē] When someone does tai chi, he or she is doing special Chinese exercises to make the mind and body stronger. **The *tai chi* class is fun.**

English-Language Arts Content Standards

 **READING**

1.0 **Word Analysis, Fluency, and Systematic Vocabulary Development**
Students understand the basic features of reading. They select letter patterns and know how to translate them into spoken language by using phonics, syllabication, and word parts. They apply this knowledge to achieve fluent oral and silent reading.

Decoding and Word Recognition

1.1 Recognize and use knowledge of spelling patterns (e.g., diphthongs, special vowel spellings) when reading.

1.2 Apply knowledge of basic syllabication rules when reading (e.g., vowel-consonant-vowel = *su/per*; vowel-consonant/consonant-vowel = *sup/per*).

1.3 Decode two-syllable nonsense words and regular multisyllable words.

1.4 Recognize common abbreviations (e.g., *Jan.*, *Sun.*, *Mr.*, *St.*).

1.5 Identify and correctly use regular plurals (e.g., *-s*, *-es*, *-ies*) and irregular plurals (e.g., *fly/flies*, *wife/wives*).

1.6   Read aloud fluently and accurately and with appropriate intonation and expression.

Vocabulary and Concept Development

1.7   Understand and explain common antonyms and synonyms.

1.8   Use knowledge of individual words in unknown compound words to predict their meaning.

1.9   Know the meaning of simple prefixes and suffixes (e.g., *over-*, *un-*, *-ing*, *-ly*).

1.10   Identify simple multiple-meaning words.

2.0   Reading Comprehension

Students read and understand grade-level-appropriate material. They draw upon a variety of comprehension strategies as needed (e.g., generating and responding to essential questions, making predictions, comparing information from several sources). The selections in *Recommended Literature, Kindergarten Through Grade Twelve* illustrate the quality and complexity of the materials to be read by students. In addition to their regular school reading, by grade four, students read one-half million words annually, including a good representation of grade-level-appropriate narrative and expository text (e.g., classic and contemporary literature, magazines, newspapers, online information). In grade two, students continue to make progress toward this goal.

Structural Features of Informational Materials

2.1   Use titles, tables of contents, and chapter headings to locate information in expository text.

Comprehension and Analysis of Grade-Level-Appropriate Text

2.2   State the purpose in reading (i.e., tell what information is sought).

2.3   Use knowledge of the author's purpose(s) to comprehend informational text.

2.4   Ask clarifying questions about essential textual elements of exposition (e.g., *why*, *what if*, *how*).

2.5   Restate facts and details in the text to clarify and organize ideas.

2.6   Recognize cause-and-effect relationships in a text.

2.7   Interpret information from diagrams, charts, and graphs.

2.8   Follow two-step written instructions.

3.0 Literary Response and Analysis

Students read and respond to a wide variety of significant works of children's literature. They distinguish between the structural features of the text and the literary terms or elements (e.g., theme, plot, setting, characters). The selections in *Recommended Literature, Kindergarten Through Grade Twelve* illustrate the quality and complexity of the materials to be read by students.

Narrative Analysis of Grade-Level-Appropriate Text

3.1 Compare and contrast plots, settings, and characters presented by different authors.

3.2 Generate alternative endings to plots and identify the reason or reasons for, and the impact of, the alternatives.

3.3 Compare and contrast different versions of the same stories that reflect different cultures.

3.4 Identify the use of rhythm, rhyme, and alliteration in poetry.

 WRITING

1.0 Writing Strategies

Students write clear and coherent sentences and paragraphs that develop a central idea. Their writing shows they consider the audience and purpose.

Students progress through the stages of the writing process (e.g., prewriting, drafting, revising, editing successive versions).

Organization and Focus

1.1 Group related ideas and maintain a consistent focus.

Penmanship

1.2 Create readable documents with legible handwriting.

Research

1.3 Understand the purposes of various reference materials (e.g., dictionary, thesaurus, atlas).

Evaluation and Revision

1.4 Revise original drafts to improve sequence and provide more descriptive detail.

2.0 **Writing Applications (Genres and Their Characteristics)**
Students write compositions that describe and explain familiar objects, events, and experiences. Student writing demonstrates a command of standard American English and the drafting, research, and organizational strategies outlined in Writing Standard 1.0.

Using the writing strategies of grade two outlined in Writing Standard 1.0, students:

2.1 Write brief narratives based on their experiences:

　　　a. Move through a logical sequence of events.

　　　b. Describe the setting, characters, objects, and events in detail.

2.2 Write a friendly letter complete with the date, salutation, body, closing, and signature.

 WRITTEN AND ORAL ENGLISH LANGUAGE CONVENTIONS

The standards for written and oral English language conventions have been placed between those for writing and for listening and speaking because these conventions are essential to both sets of skills.

1.0 **Written and Oral English Language Conventions**
Students write and speak with a command of standard English conventions appropriate to this grade level.

Sentence Structure

1.1 Distinguish between complete and incomplete sentences.

1.2 Recognize and use the correct word order in written sentences.

Grammar

1.3   Identify and correctly use various parts of speech, including nouns and verbs, in writing and speaking.

Punctuation

1.4   Use commas in the greeting and closure of a letter and with dates and items in a series.

1.5   Use quotation marks correctly.

Capitalization

1.6   Capitalize all proper nouns, words at the beginning of sentences and greetings, months and days of the week, and titles and initials of people.

Spelling

1.7   Spell frequently used, irregular words correctly (e.g., *was, were, says, said, who, what, why*).

1.8   Spell basic short-vowel, long-vowel, *r*-controlled, and consonant-blend patterns correctly.

1.0   Listening and Speaking Strategies
Students listen critically and respond appropriately to oral communication. They speak in a manner that guides the listener to understand important ideas by using proper phrasing, pitch, and modulation.

Comprehension

1.1   Determine the purpose or purposes of listening (e.g., to obtain information, to solve problems, for enjoyment).

1.2   Ask for clarification and explanation of stories and ideas.

1.3   Paraphrase information that has been shared orally by others.

1.4   Give and follow three- and four-step oral directions.

Organization and Delivery of Oral Communication

1.5   Organize presentations to maintain a clear focus.

1.6   Speak clearly and at an appropriate pace for the type of communication (e.g., informal discussion, report to class).

1.7   Recount experiences in a logical sequence.

1.8 Retell stories, including characters, setting, and plot.

1.9 Report on a topic with supportive facts and details.

2.0 **Speaking Applications (Genres and Their Characteristics)**

Students deliver brief recitations and oral presentations about familiar experiences or interests that are organized around a coherent thesis statement. Student speaking demonstrates a command of standard American English and the organizational and delivery strategies outlined in Listening and Speaking Standard 1.0.

Using the speaking strategies of grade two outlined in Listening and Speaking Standard 1.0, students:

2.1 Recount experiences or present stories:

　a. Move through a logical sequence of events.

　b. Describe story elements (e.g., characters, plot, setting).

2.2 Report on a topic with facts and details, drawing from several sources of information.

Acknowledgments

For permission to reprint copyrighted material, grateful acknowledgment is made to the following sources:

Capstone Press: From *Goods and Services* by Janeen R. Adil. Text copyright © 2006 by Capstone Press. From *Scarcity* by Janeen R. Adil. Text © 2006 by Capstone Press.

Compass Point Books: From *Law and Order* by David Conrad. Text © 2003 by Compass Point Books.

HarperCollins Publishers: From *Lemonade for Sale* by Stuart J. Murphy, illustrated by Tricia Tusa. Text copyright © 1998 by Stuart J. Murphy; illustrations copyright © 1998 by Tricia Tusa. From *From Seed to Pumpkin* by Wendy Pfeffer, illustrated by James Graham Hale. Text copyright © 2004 by Wendy Pfeffer; illustrations copyright © 2004 by James Graham Hale.

Millbrook Press, a division of Lerner Publishing Group, Inc.: From *Grandma Lai Goon Remembers* by Ann Morris, illustrated by Peter Linenthal. Text copyright © 2002 by Ann Morris. Photographs and illustrations © 2002 by Peter Linenthal.

Sasquatch Books: The Giant Cabbage: An Alaskan Folktale by Chérie B. Stihler, illustrated by Jeremiah Trammell. Text copyright © 2003 by Chérie B. Stihler; illustrations copyright © 2003 by Jeremiah Trammell.

Scholastic Inc.: "The Ant and the Grasshopper" and cover illustration by Gilles from *Aesop's Fables*, retold by Ann McGovern. Text and cover illustration copyright © 1963 by Scholastic Inc. Published by Scholastic Apple Classics.